Alchemy of
Scallops

Alchemy of
Scallops

REBA OWEN

Cover photo by Sarah Owen
Back photo by Nikki Rusinovich

ISBN: Softcover   978-1-5144-8639-9
               eBook   978-1-5144-8638-2

Print information available on the last page.

Rev. date: 05/03/2016

To order additional copies of this book, contact:
Xlibris
1-888-795-4274
www.Xlibris.com
Orders@Xlibris.com
738627

Contents

When I see Ravens, I think of you; smart, wise, clever, and raucous when upset. But always one step ahead of the rest of us.

Dudley Nelson
10/13/2015

Dedication

To Anna, Chase, Nikki and Shane

The Alchemy of Scallops

A scallop shell, golden and iridescent like Rapunzel's tresses.
One black with white and orange mottling, a Japanese fan
that a rice-pale geisha would have peered from behind.
The next a golden cream with an edge pattern of cinnamon,
with which a duchess might fan herself at a soiree'.
The large speckled, marked with orderly Indian corn lines
Its companion a sand colored shell scarred with grooves,
from a burrowing marine worm,
bringing to mind a mesa's eroded face.
There is another the color of noon sun on beach grass.
And one, opaque with muted lavender edging, a sunset ending.
Finally a tiny scallop, the size and blush of a baby's toe.
Some little ghost-pale piece of flesh created these from sea water,
to amaze with the mystery of its alchemy that we humans are not,
and never will be capable of.

Reba Owen
1/28/2014
Sunset Beach, California

Winter Wren Christmas Morning

Drab and cinnamon like dead leaves and dirt.
Shy about the tangled twigs and thicket.
Her quivering throat the only clue to her disguise.
A winter wren, her song joyous and honeyed.

Who can be sad when she sings?
Who, in agony over wanting those back
who have gone to that soil, cannot be cheered?
Who, though grieving loving words said too late,
would not be soothed by her tremolo?

And who, cannot look forward as her little aria
leads the way to a new dawn on the frost laden forest?

Reba Owen
2014

Signs of Insanity

It all started with drowned bees. Honey bees had gotten into the hummingbird feeder. As I was cleaning their bodies out of the container in the kitchen sink, their feelers began moving, then their wings. Horrified, I put the six of them on a paper towel in a small dry gift box, along with some Christmas Roses. Because of the temperature drop outside I decided to wait to release the bees until it was warmer. But, they would have to be fed. I put a bit of honey on the end of a tooth pick and offered it to one of the patients. Sure enough, its tiny mouth parts seemed to be tasting the offering. That was the start of my considering I might be insane.

A month earlier I saw a woman my age (old) with heavy floral tattoos on her arms. She was at the supermarket down the aisle from me in the vegetable department. Mentally I though, now that just looks awful! What could she have been thinking? Suddenly she was coming closer as if she could read my thoughts. When she passed, I saw that the "tattoos" were actually a rose design on her long sleeved blouse. At that point I hadn't considered the insanity possibility, just aging eyesight.

However, I was at the store to buy a metal water bottle to keep in my car. One of my resolves being to drink more water. In the ensuing weeks the water from this bottle tasted awful, an iodine flavor. On the label it said "Product of China". Perhaps by soaking the container for a few days, the taste would disappear. Well, the taste did disappear. When I dumped the soaking water, the product pamphlet, all soggy, came out of the bottle. At that point, the possibility of a problem started to form. And don't worry, I will get back to the bee story shortly.

My cousins' were having a holiday soiree on their houseboat. As I was coming down the long ramp an older gentleman passed me and nodded "Good Evening". He smelled good! Oh my, I thought, I like that smell. As I got further down the ramp the smell wafted out behind him even stronger. It got stronger and stronger. I soon realized it was someone's dryer vent.

I kept the bee's in their box for 3 days until the sun came out. I released them to some heather that was in full, winter bloom. Later in the day, they were gone.

What does any of this have to do with insanity, you might ask? Well prior to all these incidents I had been contacted, on Facebook, by my old college boyfriend. His longtime wife had died. He lived across the country. We visited on the phone and caught up on the last 52 years. After college he tried to visit me once but I was already involved with my husband to be, and on the verge of 40 years of a tempestuous married life, which ended in divorce. Yesterday I began thinking, what if I had it to do over again? What if I had chosen differently all those years ago? And knowing what I know now, whom would I choose today? Insane or not insane? My answer to myself proves it.

Thirty Days into Winter

"Forellenschluss" is an heirloom lettuce,
rosette of bright green leaves splashed with maroon,
and a smooth buttery flavor, a German name meaning
"speckled trout back".
Winter is forgotten between the mail box and the dining room,
where garden catalogs reign and rule their kingdom of hope.
My neighbor asks that I gather their mail for a few days.
Her husband, who has to get to a heart surgeon
100 miles away, just left in an ambulance, lights flashing.
The wife hopes for divine intervention for her minister husband,
who conceivably has more credibility that most.
Our gardens are old lake beds, rich in humus, and plant fossils
long disintegrated. We are all disintegrating slowly, some with passion
some without, and some with no choice.

Reba Owen
1/18/2014

Mirror in the Dark

Stored in a closet, the walnut frame dulled
with webs of house spiders and the dust of lives.
The imagined images there
layered one on another.
A carriage cloak trimmed in fox,
grey eyes and black ringlets,
a favored hound,
snow on oaks through a frosted window,
layered one on another.
Strung pink pearls from Bora Bora,
jade lotus comb from a Shanghai tomb,
mourning necklace of human hair,
then dark on dark,
layered one on another.

Until today when suddenly, sunlight pierces
the mirror and scatters the guardian spiders.

Reba Owen
2/24/2014

Wild Plums

A winter of world news
too terrible to put on paper,
and months of mundane sadnesses,
reports and biopsies,
friendships rent,
brakes and shattered glass,
unexplained forgetting.

Amid the black spruce shadows
the wild plums appear
blossoms white or cream
a living Chinese tapestry.
They appear year after year
to pull their sugar from the
still frosty soil.

And I remember then,
some Septembers,
fishing the green Deschutes
and a basket with that scarlet jelly
and Indian fry bread.

On Ice

The racer
Yankee Clipper,
hangs in the basement
dusty and cobweb draped,
youth hanging there,
varnished maple slats
red runners burnished silver
from the last ice storm
seven years ago.
That's when I went
okole over teakettle
down an embankment,
injured three ribs from laughter,
and was put on orders
by Him.

January Lake

There is a man lying at the bottom of the January lake.
The helicopter spotlight is gone.
The blue police skiff is gone.
The red lights flashing off the yellow fire coats are gone.
The dark figures of neighbors are back in their homes,
porch lights off, one by one.
Even the shrouded moon has sunk into the sea.

Tomorrow the divers will come,
and search the thick blankets of milfoil and fan wort.
The bass will flee .... not understanding.

Reba Owen
1/17/2016

Haiku

Jungle of lupine
in the vernal rain concrete
all is possible.

Senryu

Wrist jagged white scar
vicious attack assailant
sharp thorn yellow rose.

-escence

whenever the west wind blows
the scents of lavender
and lily of the valley
ascend and remind
of a childhood free of worry
about what time it was,
and if the moon would fail to rise,
when decisions were things
that other people made among
the fringe cups and not-to-pick trilliums,
all competing for bees and beetles,
while I wandered oblivious
to all that was bad around me.
Those woods seem so far away now.

Reba Owen
5/13/2013

Hellebores

They flower from the winter floor,
"food for fawns" in Greek.
Petals of nectar while bees still sleep.
Sepals veined and splashed with rose,
the darkest like Alexander's
maroon cape and crest.
The whitest, as pale as his brow
when twelve days he lay dying.
Such beauty said to summon demons.
Such beauty said to rescue the daughter's of Midas
as they ran naked and screaming through the streets of Argos.
Such beauty.

Jennie's Quarry

From a limestone pit and cement fortune,
grew the garden Jennie envisioned,
a thousand horse carts of farmland soil
brought in to blanket the exhausted quarry.
All seasons reflected in ponds and fountains,
petals and paths winding to amazement,
scene after scene. Wisteria and roses racing
each other to bloom. The air filled with scents
of alyssum, honeysuckle, and violets.
The Japanese garden, formal and exquisitely bare,
with a moon window cut in a hawthorn hedge.
Through its opening a view of a private cove of green water,
in miniature, a sloop tied to a mossy dock.
A small plot of giants, gunnera and bayonet-like New Zealand flax
dinosaurs of the plant world.
All around the sound of water gurgling, rivuleting, sparrow splashing.
A begonia bower, huge pendulous blooms like confections of cake
frosting
rose, pink and salmon.
But the crème de la crème,
blue Himalayan poppies, pieces of sky fallen to earth.

Reba Owen
3/25/2013

1948

1948 was the year I decided to trap the Easter Bunny. That rabbit, the bearer of chocolate, was an important part of my childhood, along with Santa Claus, fairies, witches, ghosts, Frankenstein, and Dracula.

Someone like Dracula would be easy to recognize. If you couldn't tell by his odd clothes, all you had to do was look into his eyes. Instead of pupils there would be flapping bats. The Easter Bunny problem was more difficult. He came at night while you slept, and hid your basket of goodies somewhere in the house. In our rural neighborhood there were lots of rabbits. Unlike Santa or Dracula, no one knew where the Easter Bunny lived.

It would be necessary to trap him in the house, better yet, in my own bedroom. The plan was not to harm him, but to verify his existence. Perhaps I would stroke his back and scratch behind his ears as I often did with my cat, Snoopy. Then I would allow him to go his way.

The only part of the plan I divulged to my parents and siblings was that I would leave a carrot in my room for our Easter visitor. The part about sprinkling flour all over the hard-wood floor in my room, was known to me alone. Several times before falling asleep, I listened and looked out my window. Starlight reflected on the river and lawn. Shadows became shapes that seemed to move. Some forms had ears, I thought.

In the morning, the carrots were half eaten. Rabbit-like tracks in the flour led to and from the bait. Trapping the Easter Bunny cured my inquisitive nature for some time. My parents never said a thing about the incident, other than asking me to sweep up the flour I had "somehow" spilled in my room.

Christmas 1948 brought the annual visit to Meier and Frank's Department Store to sit on Santa's lap. As I walked down the red carpet toward Santa, he pointed at me and said loudly, "Oh here's the little girl who tried to trap the Easter Bunny." It took a long time for my mom, grandma, Santa, and the floor manager to quell my guilty sobbing.

By my thirties, I had transitioned from actual entities to the "spirit" of Santa, Easter Rabbit, and Dracula. My own children visited Santa at the shopping mall, but asked first why Santa had a plaid, blue shirt-sleeve showing from under his suit. And it was in my thirties that I asked my Dad about the Easter Bunny tracks in the flour.

He said, "I had a terrible time getting your cat, Snoopy, to hold still and be quiet while I pressed her feet in your trap."

Reba Owen
1997 (revised 2007)

Things Remembered from Spring

Pollen exploding from the pine tree
onto the full flesh of magnolias.
The neighbor boy, with his hair slicked back,
cards pinned to his bicycle spokes,
doing wheelies on the road.
The cattailed ditches.
The vernal pools with frogs
calling their hunger.
The salamanders slipping
about in their water ballets.
Bumble bees still in winter stupor,
rising from their burrows.
Now
playing a song I didn't know then,
"Can't Help But Wonder Where I'm Bound."

Reba Owen
3/15/2015

Eclipse

The dark brush cracks and creaks
as the eclipse sneaks
forward and suddenly
rises from the side of
Neahkahnie like burnt orange
science fiction.
Lemon from cusp to cusp.
Saturn dangles just below
while Venus on high south
glows like a bleached clam shell.

The Mascon in the Mare Frigoris

Fired by e-mail in the middle of the night
from a toxic job that
was like a mascon, that invisible tether, gravitational pull
slowing cutting into ankle and skull,
a decade in the making.
Women are supposed to support their kind,
but vipers have no such code.
Should I send them an e-mail
with the first swallowtail I saw today,
so they would bite themselves in anger?

*Mare Frigoris means "Sea of Cold". Mascons are impact areas of
metorites on the moon, that have heavier gravitational pulls. (Newly
discovered 2013) Early astronomers thought the dark spaces on the
moon were seas)

Ode To Chickweed

Chickweed, fragile as down
on birdlets so named.
(Stellaria media) seeded as silt.
Before the gardener knows
the chickweed sows its children
while aunts and uncles, cousins too,
crowd the hostas, cloak violas, then
quietly and patiently
mate again, to launch
new families.
Oh yes, the gardener easily
pulls the chickweed from the earth.
It fakes screams
decibels from our range.
The gardener hangs up the hoe,
puts gloves to rest, smug and confident
of the battle won,
while patiently the chickweed waits
until the (home sapiens) has gone inside.

Time Vesper

Curvature of the moon
Always changing, always the same,
Let us observe before we sleep.
Every flower fattening seed,
No cloud too plain.
Delay your racing.
As each day passes,
Release your heart to something ....

Yellow Fish

Yellow fish with lemony scales
swim west of a rocky shoal.
Go west young fish, go west,
like me .... fins fanning,
trying to stay upright,
knowing where air is and water ends.
No sounds in the submerging
but taste and smell swirl.
Hued plastics glow and beguile
rainbow metals blind the fish,
or hypnotize,
like the five mirrors in my way.

Reba Owen
10/08/2012

Winter Fire

The owl lightly brushes the spruce.
A fine dust of minute ice crystals
cascades to the lower branches.
The full moon is rising, tree-framed, in the east.
Cold is forming the first skim on my lake,
and I think of a time in another place
when my father took us skating.
The ice so thick, he was able
to build a fire on the surface of the lake.
Even now in this cold,
I am warmed by that long ago fire.

Reba Owen
11/15/2015

B Flat

As I have said many times while forming the hated B flat:
why can't all songs be written in the minor chords of which
Am is the greatest, most exquisite, with hand maidens Dm and Cm?
Other musicians often disagree. They point out that B flat is the sound
of a lanyard
clinking in the breeze against a metal flag pole by a green lake. It is the
sound of a mailbox closing after one retrieves a valentine. Or a seat buckle
against the
door when one steps out to view the blue sea.
Is it not the sound they say, of a fork hitting a plate after a piece of tiramisu?
The key turning in your lock after a safe journey home?
And what about the latch sound of the garden gate?
The garden with its bachelor buttons, goedicia, sweet peas, Queen Ann's
Lace,
and trumpet flowers ; trumpet flowers whose B flats are at an octave
audible only to
themselves.

Migration of Snow Drops

A water fall of white spills down a verdant bank,
(Antidote to Circe's poison and intoxicant to ants.)
These are not the ancient blooms here on the river's edge.
The marriage of fleeing winter and rushing spring,
brings a question who and when birthed these pendants
on this hillside where cars now flash by, oblivious.

Perhaps a scientist could formulate the speed
with which these lovelies are moving,
and calculate in decimals their slow descent
by offset bulblets and ant carried seed.

The Sunflower Sea Star

Twenty-armed, graceful, elegant
like rose-purple aliens in still tide pools.
They move with tube feet over sand and stone
sprinters of the starfish clan
searching for something to embrace.
All in their path, mussels, urchins, abalone
succumb to the hypnotizing flower vision,
unaware of the potent danger,
the stars' gelatinous stomach enveloping
the victim's unsuspecting body.
The Sunflower star having dissolved its prey
moves on, much as some humans
tend to do,
don't you think?

Reba Owen
8/27/2013

Wings

On the windowsill a crane fly body lies.
The fragile wings hypnotize,
an amnesic millisecond of forgetting.
Forgetting a tumor spread from tongue to jaw,
surgeons carving,
harvest of leg bone and veins,
transfusion after transfusion.

In life the filaments formed a geometric map,
a network for protein and sugar,
calligraphy curving and fine,
supporting the wing which
under glass shimmers purple,
like the last line of a sunset,
or a cathedral window in miniature.

Tide

Frost is on the heather
despite the golden winter day.
The lip on combers
flash in the drowning sun.
I am in the last season of a century
and trying to explain that I do not wish
to conform to anything.
Feelings, are my core of being
as is lack of feelings should I choose.
On the water surfers are languid,
waiting for the right wave.
Regret washes over me that I am not out there,
and never will be.
But later when the tide is neap,
and the quarter moon is up,
there is no cold in my solitude
only the warmth of freedom.

Reba Owen
11/24/2013

Season of Grasses

Feathered and plumed, the grasses are flesh,
laden with ripeness, bread on the wind.
Florets in minutia, stolons and whorls,
Gramineae whose phytoliths sparkle and twirl.
We who came fifty-five million years later,
turned the monocots to whiskey,
and scaffolds, and woodwinds whose sweet notes
split the air with anthems and hymns.

We came and groomed the grasses never to seed
in velvet shroud around flat stones
over bones of our righteousness and greed.

Reba Owen
6/7/2011

The Mountain

As a child I swam in Spirit Lake at the base of the volcano, Mt. St. Helens. There were trees upright, under the water, ghosts from some ancient cataclysmic event. It was a spooky place, where loons cried and owls called. At night, fog in the moonlight, rose in eerie swaying shapes.

When the mountain went off again, I drove to Woodland to get a closer look. My seven year-old granddaughter had helped me figure out my digital camera. Sixteen years ago, in the big eruption, the ash fall blew south, smothering my new cucumber plants. We put pantyhose over the car air filter. Pharmacies sold out of surgical masks. Children and pets stayed indoors. Fortunately, this time the ash was blowing north.

The drive itself was green and rolling, maples turning spring yellow, fields of mustard and wild radish. The weather was partly cloudy. I couldn't see the mountain, but a large ash plume was roiling upward in the distance.

I found a muddy turn-out by a farm field, pulled over, got out, and began snapping pictures. "What a National Geographic moment," I thought. Across the field I saw a man approaching. A farmer perhaps.

"What are you doing?" He said.

"I hope I'm not trespassing ...... I'm filming the mountain. It's going off you know."

"Well, I hate to tell you this, missy but that's not the volcano. You're filming the Camas Pulp Mill."

"Oh no!"

"Oh yes. Don't feel bad, you're not the only one." Said the farmer.

Reba Owen 2006

An Observance of Silence

Holding a handful of scallop shells
caramel, beige, maroon and cream
each pattern of ribs mathematically arranged,
little timeless fans of calcium and lime,
from beaches north and beaches south
each shell speaking a different dialect,
Tlingit, Maori, Chinook, Tongan, Pennacook.
Their like designs earthen and geometric
on basket dreams and beadwork,
cedar panels, tapa cloth, and canoes.
Where flesh was, I touch the shallow cup,
smooth and quiet,
no sound of the surf.

Mariposa Road

(Ode to Robert and Thea)

The saffron tips of willows along the bay
are the only warmth coloring January.
January all grey and gray outside.
I am reading the Mariposa Road
by the fire.
Wings of blue iridescence and orchid edging,
yellow orange tips, cloud white sulfurs, four-spots
with black bodies and scarlet heads. Fritillaries spotted amber and gold.

They appear in mind, of course, but then fly to the milkweed
sprouting from the carpet which then becomes a mass of
sky-colored lupines and verbena.
Huge green moths emerge from moon flowers
that have opened on the ceiling. Suddenly, a squadron of swallowtails
fills the room, so many that the slight breeze from their wings
creates a wind that rushes up the chimney, drawing my thoughts
out into the mist.
The saffron willows are ready for a change in season,
and so am I.

Earth Day

4/22/2013

The first tern has arrived
white and gleaming as if she rose
from the morning shimmer on the bay
and not the quiet shoals of Mexico.

Animalia chordata ave
Charadriiform lari sterna

And on Earth Day as if
she were a sentinel,
chosen to remind all,
drowning in blood and sorrow.

Animalia chordata ave
Charadriiform lari sterna

Rising high, hovering, eye never wavering
to plummet for prey below,
the silver cloud unawares
before they join the cycle.

Animalia chordata ave
Charadriiform lari sterna, Spero.

Reba Owen
4/22/2013

* Spero (Latin for hope)

Moon Sonnet

I'm in love with the moon
drinking up the sea,
while all the night owls croon
he looks down on me.
Sometimes he's warm and summer soft
rising oe'r the lake,
but in winter he is ice aloft
indifferent to me awake.
I'm in love with the man in the sky
so far and yet so near
bathed in that ivory light on high
unreachable I do fear.
Perhaps we are the perfect pair.
Lovers, faithful, always there.

Reba Owen
6/8/2013

October Sun

The day after cards and cake,
the October sun hypnotizes: this scene will continue
despite the morning frost.
A crow is scolding some enemy in the spruce,
a stellar meowing like a cat.
Even leaf smoke and the blower next door
is soothing in a strange sort of manner.
We are all winterizing, aren't we?
I am, but in a different way, here in the warmth
not knowing how long.
Ritual by ritual,
hoping forever,
recognizing that is foolish.
Ritual by ritual... pumpkins ready for carving,
cider chilling,
a black plastic rat on the door step
next to yellow and white mums.
Mocky's leaf patterned bowl full of candy corn.
But for this moment in the October sun,
I do not wish for anyone to snap their fingers.

Reba Owen
10/14/2013

Thoughts on the Last Day of Fall

The bay flats are silvered and blue,
reflecting the glow after sunset.
The moon full and rising, the last moon of autumn
falling into winter, and I am fighting the sadness of the season.
Without reason it appears even in this iridescent scene.
The bare branches of oak, alder, birch and wild pear
seem to be grasping the quickly appearing stars.

It is time then, to get a box down from cupboard.
A bell made from a can lid at camp (won in a swimming contest on a
summer lake).
A barn owl feather from a courting walk along the Tillamook.
Glass icicles that hung fifty years on the parent's tree.
A star of Reynolds Wrap, made for me when I had nothing.
Frogs, birds, foxes, Santas, cats, butterflies, chipmunks, mice, deer,
rainbows of
glass balls, nests, sparkly mushrooms, mini-paper-Victorian houses
covered in snow,
and a crystal snowflake that you gave me, once ....
The scent of cedar and fir, cinnamon and oranges, and the path of the
moon
on its way to the new year.

Reba Owen
11/26/2012

Heirlooms

```
                f
   it      a
   is      e
   it      l
   is
```

a melody on the wind, sugar songs
golden tones of orange pippin and honey-
crisp, jonathan, brandywine and northern spy.
gargantuan wolf rivers, tiny saffron spitzenbergs
gravensteins, ashmead's kernel, brandy wine, pearl
braeburn, bramley, mcintosh, all sweet with water
spots and cider dreams. gala from the roaring 20
granny smith, cortlands, transparent yellows
mutsu, fuji, ginger gold, gordon, gold rush.
winter bananna, spartan, red rome.
but hidden in a beverly hills
Eris spreads her discord
with gilted codling
worms worms

Reba Owen
10/15/2012

Night Rescues

A night terror woke me,
I was in Bangkok without a ticket
or a passport, when really the Oregon rain
played a safe sonata on the bedroom window.
Or the night, deep in REM sleep,
a gaboon viper bit my hand, my scream sending
the cat soaring off the bed, and into the soft
patterns of the moonlight on the rug.
How many times a childhood dream revisits:
on the river bank by a huge fir tree,
a crack forms behind me, the tree shudders and
starts to fall ..... I awake, saved because
starlight is sparkling in the hemlock branches outside,
and the quip-quip of a night hawk is calling me.

Reba Owen
3/17/2013

Ripppet Road

Ripppet Road is swampy
and was named by numerous frogs
who live along its edges.
Did they think that name would prevent
pickups with bloodied elk carcasses
from spraying gravel on their smooth green heads?
Or did the croakers wish to hear the murmur
of children repeating and repeating a similar sound,
that the frogs make themselves?
The county did not wish to have amphibians
naming roads. But the web footed ones hired an attorney
and prevailed over Gramson Way.

Revenge

First there was pain and then the fullness of blood in my sandal. The sundial was sticking in my foot as I hopped around in the dark trying to kick it loose as if it were a Tasmanian devil or bear trap. The small bronze sundial with its bloodied pointer finally shook loose and clattered on the garden stones. I am most embarrassed to say that I was out in the garden at 11 pm dispatching slugs. I only went to the hospital emergency at midnight because my tetanus shot was out of date. The thought of my body constricting into a backward u position and my breathing shutting off, literally terrified me. The night receptionist said, "You have 72 hours after an injury to get a tetanus shot". (Google said to get help right away if you are worried). I felt Google was a better authority than a receptionist with 20 years experience so I insisted on being seen. She called back to the inner sanctum. "Patient with sun dial attack!" When the nurse came out he gave it a different spin. Slug Revenge uh? I never did see a doctor but the nice nurse, sort of a handsome surfer dude cleaned the wound and gave me a DPT shot. Will the DP part hurt me at my age I asked? Probably he said but you won't get tetanus. I was cured not only of possible tetanus but also of impaling any more slugs. I switched to beer.

Reminder

In the wind the lanyard and flagpole
Have harmonized in unison,
Each together sending notes across the green lake.
A cat collar and bicycle bell
Ring sweet warnings
Making trills as surely as a flute or triangle.
Under the moon a cricket,
Sure of her aria to the evening,
Is a reminder of an old song,
Chords and lyrics of Loesser and Lane.

Reba Owen 9/17/2013

Whirlwind

The other seasons come in softly, respectfully,
Winter, an exquisite snow flake appears from a grey sky.
Spring, a miniscule green bud or snowdrop beckons.
Summer, a tiger swallowtail floats by.
But fall arrives in a whirlwind,
a vortex of leaves and limbs, confetti of petals, and
overturned pots.
Records shatter, allowing salmon to rush in waters
that a day before were too shallow to pass.
Mosses, like chameleons, change from brown to green.
Pumpkins orange and white materialize from their jungle of vines.
The next evening as if nothing has happened, Venus shines
her a crystal light in the west. The geese honk south under Aquarius,
and in the darkness a doe seeks out red apples littering the ground.
Tomorrow I will rescue all the green tomatoes.

Reba Owen
10/1/2013

The Full Crow Moon

The full crow moon rises tonight
over hills and woodlands
still folded in the dark shadows,
where fiddle neck ferns are peeking from leaf mold,
and black tree frogs sing their way to green.
High in the firs the crows slumber,
fluffed against the frosty shimmer of moonlight,
and the soft padding of the fox.
When daylight comes
the crows click and caw
loud and brash
that all should know
the vernal equinox.

The Gardeners Next Door

Doctor Wilson, the obstetrician
cared for begonias and women's woes,
like fine pastries and confections all.
His paths were lined with magnolias,
white and lush as throats and thighs,
while his own wife was plain and brown as dust.
He just fell asleep, dreaming of lace and laughter.

Tony, the policeman,
grew com as tall as firs and steeples,
covered with kernels that popped on touch.
A fungus from Guadalcanal filled his stomach
until he was dead.
Undaunted, his wife kept him in ajar
rather than spread him in the rows as he had wanted.

Frank, the electrician,
trained and trimmed his nectar berries and wives.
One day he short-circuited, chased his fourth
with a sharpened hoe
past the sumptuous red and gold snapdragons,
and scared all the children playing in the street.
No one knows what happened after that.

Ken, the bar pilot,
grafted pink and white hawthorn on the same tree
and asked what did we think about this and that
while he staked his dahlias big as a plate
and voted no on each tax rate
until his kidneys, misdiagnosed
did him in.

Grampa Fred, the Navy man,
grew peace roses big as cabbages.
Filbert and red winter pears soldiered through his field.
When cancer rescued him from the veterans' home,
his belongings were shared equally among the heirs,
except for a squabble over a maple nutcracker
in the shape of a nude woman.

Reba Owen
05/21/2013

Youngs Bay Metaphor

Some think the strands of sunlight are from god.
This morning these bands make a glittering pattern
on the surface of the bay.
Fish from everywhere race to the reflection,
assuming bait food are floundering there
in the changing tide.
Some fish flash away in disgust at the mirage,
while others linger, finding comfort
for their cold and hungry scales.

In Country

How far would stretch a women's wall
names in granite cut
deep as scars and dark as hate?
Crying vets' tears would hardly wash away
the stone and marble years.
Hah! "In Country" sure enough.
Where's the monument to rear
for those who lasted all their years
and those who fell along the way,
in country, dear?

Coda

Before Grandma died
she walked through the living room
in a Hawaiian print dress.
She was young and slender.
the scent of her pikaki lei
was like jasmine and vanilla.
It was the same one Grampa
gave her in 1938. She twirled
slowly and smiled.
She didn't see me sleeping
on the couch, or Grampa in his bed.
Breathed so easy and waved
in slow motion
like a gull's wing,
as she stepped
from her skeletal body
one last time.

Before Grandma died
she accepted Jesus,
that's what the Reverend
said of his last minute conversation
with her and the morphine.

Choice

The gauze of morning fog turns the sun to moon.
The teals and widgeons asleep,
bob on the incoming tide which is riffling the bay.
The water's movement stirs the salmon
to their upstream song.

I am looking for a sign,
going or staying,
asking, must there always be a journey?
Could one vantage be the answer
while others meander by
on their preordained paths and trails,
orbits and currents, lines and traces?

Perhaps there is no choice,
like the sumac nearby
sending its red feathers aloft
at the whim
of the first chill draft of Fall.

Reba Owen is a Northwest poet, artist, ukulele player, and boogie boarder. Her poems and art reflect a love of nature. In this book, she hopes to illustrate the ongoing wonder that is the world out of doors. She also infuses some social comments about humans and their foibles. Reba is a 1962 graduate of Oregon State University with a degree in recreation. The book is dedicated to her grandchildren, Anna, Shane, Chase, and Nikki.

In my previous book, I acknowledged all in my family, friends, mentors, teachers, fellow writers who had influenced and encouraged me. To that list I now want to add the music makers who have brought me such joy in the last couple years. You know who you are, and I love every single one of you.

Edwards Brothers Malloy
Thorofare, NJ USA
October 12, 2016